Alexa, what is there to know about love?

Also by Brian Bilston

You Took the Last Bus Home

Diary of a Somebody

Brian Bilston

Alexa, what is there to know about love?

PICADOR POETRY

First published 2021 by Picador
an imprint of Pan Macmillan
The Smithson, 6 Briset Street, London EC1M 5NR
EU representative: Macmillan Publishers Ireland Limited,
Mallard Lodge, Lansdowne Village, Dublin 4
Associated companies throughout the world
www.panmacmillan.com

ISBN 978-1-5290-5162-9

A CIP catalogue record for this book is available from the British Library.

Printed and bound by CPI Group (UK) Ltd, Croydon, CR0 4YY

Visit **www.picador.com** to read more about all our books
and to buy them. You will also find features, author interviews and
news of any author events, and you can sign up for e-newsletters
so that you're always first to hear about our new releases.

Contents

I

II

III

IV

I

The Caveman's Lament

me think about her when sun rises
me think about her when sun sets
me say to her how much me love her
she tell me love invent not yet

me make cave all warm and cosy
me lie bearskin on cave floor
me play song of love on bone flute
she choose cave of Tim next door

me no more go out hunt mammoth
me throw spear too short or long
me sit in cave me paint her picture
she say me got perspective wrong

me cook meal to show me love her –
diplodocus with fried beans –
she say food anachronistic
but me not know what this means

stone age mighty hard for lovers
yet rub two flints look what you get
small sparks lead to big inferno
but she say love invent not yet

The Erotic Shards of Hermaclides of Thrace[*]

1 I confess I did tremble,
    for even the stiffest of branches
    must quiver
    with the first drops of rain
5 after a long summer drought.

    The Eastern wind,
    no less than the mighty Euros himself,
    carried you gently to me,
    whispering your name
10 among the dripping leaves.

    O what love we made!
    For you were not of mortal descent
    but
        like a
15 I showed you my

[*] Hermaclides of Thrace (c.680–625BC) was one of the great erotic poets of ancient Greece. Famed for the explicitness of his verse, he is thought to have written more than 15,000 lines of poetry. Sadly, all that remains are these fragments here – 32 lines and a mere 132 words – painstakingly assembled from the broken shards of a third-century BC Thessalian pot.

and, in return, you opened your
          and let me
To gaze on such magnificence!
In a frenzy, we began to
20   until

          engorged
               became moist
          as sweet as peach juice
               and down your thighs.
25 We lay there

          while still stroking each other's
               and gasping like
until we heard the angry shouts
of Zeus, your father.
30 I fled across the field in terror,

clutching my shrivelled
32 and my vestments.

Mrs Plato

'Hard day at the agora?' I asked him
as he polished off his supper.
I could sense him eyeing me nervously.
There were chickpeas in his beard again.

Earlier, he'd put his hands down his tunic
and whipped out – with a flourish –
a crumpled white rose
so I could tell something was up.

'I've been thinking . . .' he said,
(never a good sign, that) '. . . about love.'
Now this was more promising.
I adjusted my girdle.

'It's about time we moved things
to the next level,' he announced grandly.
I wondered whether I should get
the goat butter out.

But then he began to prattle
about truth and virtue and whatnot
and I thought better of it;
it goes rancid ever so quick in this heat.

I went upstairs instead and waited for him.
'There'll be none of that now,' he said
once he'd climbed in and removed my hand.
He turned away from me, untouchable,

like a newly-formed republic
asserting its independence.
I didn't cross his borders for months.
'We are trying to reach a state

beyond carnal desire,' he grumbled piously,
the night he moved himself into the spare room.
He might have been. I wasn't.
I'd had my fill of virtue.

But, by then, what did it matter?
Aristippus of Cyrene had arrived on the scene
and was busy educating me
in his own school of thought.

Five afternoons a week, in fact.
He'd knocked on my door one Tuesday
and thrust a flyer into my hand.
'Join the Hedonists!' I read.

He asked if I'd like to find out more.
'Oh, yes,' I said. 'With pleasure.'

Cleopatra

I still have it, the book we shared
(English lit, periods five and six,
each Wednesday afternoon)

in the semolina days of my youth,
when I was yellow in valour
and acned in complexion.

The desk she sat at, like a tarnished throne,
had the words 'SHAKSPEERE IS SHIT'
compass-carved into its lid.

I had immortal longings for her.
My heart was to her rubber tied by the strings:
she erased a little more of me each day.

But I was no Antony
or Craig Reynolds, for that matter.
Rumour had it they'd been spotted

behind the science labs that lunchtime
and all was lost, irretrievably.
I would build my empire in other lands.

These pages play a trick on time
and I still think of her now as she was then,
unwithered by age,

her infinite variety
never to stale by custom,
reading out loud to the rest of the class,

and that look upon her face
as she pretended to clasp the asp
to her breast.

Oh, how the boys did gasp.
Oh, how I longed to be
that asp.

Five Clerihews for Doomed Lovers

I

Pyramus and Thisbe
passing love notes on a frisbee.
Words of passion flying through the air!
Both families unaware.

II

Troilus and Cressida.
She was sad. He was wretcheder.
He went to war, with revenge to seek
because she surrendered to a Greek.

III

Petrarch and Laura.
She was already spliced when he first saw her.
He'd never quite recover from it
and would bang on about her in his sonnets.

IV

Abelard and Héloïse
caused a scandal in the diocese.
Later, she devoted herself to religious festivals.
He made do without his testicles.

V
Romeo and Juliet
must have wished they'd never met.
For what use – when dead – is love's sweet alchemy
and all that yelling from a balcony?

Drudge Work

An excerpt from Samuel Johnson's *Dictionary of the English Language*, 1st draft, 1755

LO'TTERY n. ſ. [*lotterie*, French, from *lot*.] A game of chance.

LOUD adj. 1. Noisy; striking the ear with great force.
2. Clamorous; turbulent.

LO'UDLY adv. [from *loud*.] 1. Noisy; so as to be heard far.
2. Clamorously.

LO'UDNESS n. ſ. Noise; force of sound; turbulence; furiousness of clamour.

LO'VAGE. n. ſ. [leviflicum, Latin.] A plant often used in medicine.

To LOVE. v. [lufian, Saxon.]
1. To be seized by a wild insanity.
2. To surrender all sagacity.
3. To thrash around; to be uncontrolled.
4. To feel ten years younger; or twice as old.
5. To feel diseased; to contract a pox.
6. To skip gaily through the hollyhocks.
7. To bare one's soul; to share one's heart.
8. To feel complete; to fall apart.

LOVE. n. ∫. [from the verb.]

1. A passion caused by folly or madness.

2. The arrival of a transient gladness.

3. An unwise, dangerous infatuation.

4. A non-alcoholic intoxication.

5. The romantic state of stupefaction.

6. The unhappy outcome of attraction.

7. A grim, incurable condition.

8. A word which lacks real definition.

Oh, but what balderdash and poppycock!
I blather like a bubbly-jock!
For those in search of the meaning of LOVE,
refer instead to LOTTERY (above).

Status Update: A Lonely Cloud

Status update: a lonely cloud,
As wretched as a songless thrush.
When all at once my back unbowed
To see her playing Candy Crush;
Lemonade Lake and Treacle Trees
Did dance before me in the breeze.

So vividly her sweets did shine,
A bright twinkle displaced my frown.
How gay they stretched in endless lines
To reach as far as Candy Town:
And now at last her face was seen
Reflected in her iPhone screen.

Her eyes to me were liquorice whirls,
And her skin was peppermint cream,
Her thick, thick hair did flow and swirl
Like a golden syrup'd stream.
The sweetest girl I've gazed upon!
But I could not get past level one.

Those times, when on my couch I lie
And even daffs can't lift my mood
I think back to that fine lady
Whose rare confections I'd pursued;
For then my heart with pleasure meets,
And candy-dances with her sweets.

14

Three Postcards

The first one came from Weston-super-Mare,
with the newly-built Grand Pier in view,
a bright, gleaming promise of the future,
and the sea, an impossible blue.

Unfamiliar, that neat hand, the black fountain pen.
But she knew he was the one, even then.

The next, she received eighteen months on:
Tidworth station, as viewed from Church Hill.
The foreground, a row of thatched cottages;
the barracks beyond; fields, silent and still.

She propped it against a vase on their mantelpiece,
a wedding present from her niece.

The last, a busy scene from Boulogne,
a censor-passed, heaven-sent souvenir.
'Crossing rough – but I made it!' he'd written.
When it's all over, we should come here!'

She clutched it tight as the baby moved once more.
The telegram had come two days before.

Codebreaking

Alan Turing called today.
He tells me you've got them stumped.

The boffins up at Bletchley, that is,
they've been working through their lunch-

hours, they're still hunched over
late at night. Heads down, busy grappling

with the problem that is you.
They find you maddeningly baffling,

far from breaking you, you've broken them –
they can't take it anymore.

The PM says you're distracting them
from winning us this war.

So then, what chance have I alone
of decoding all your signals?

Not a sausage. Zilch and zippo.
Or, in other words, very little.

You're an enigma, a mystery.
I'm bewildered, none the wiser.

You, with all your variations,
uncracked and undeciphered.

Minutes from a Multidisciplinary Symposium on 'What is Love?'

The philosophers claimed it all starts with Plato.
The historians showed how it's changed over time.
The chemists followed it down dopamine pathways.
The psychologists thought it was all in the mind.

The political theorists called it undemocratic.
The sociologists deemed it a social construct.
The economists said that nothing else mattered
except for how little there was, or how much.

The linguists explained how it came from Old English.
The theologians proclaimed it came straight from God.
The media studies professors weren't present
but they promised to send their thoughts in a vlog.

The anthropologists tracked its cultural rituals.
The mathematicians proved it irrational, like pi.
The art historians admired its line and perspective.
The neuroscientists traced it on brain MRIs.

The classicists found it in Cupid and Venus;
the astrophysicists, in the stars and the moon.
The musicologists plucked its song on their lute strings.
The virologists warned no one was immune.

The geographers drew up a map of its contours.
The literary theorists blamed Shakespeare and Keats.
Five days of debate, they were no nearer an answer.
The symposium resumes Wednesday next week.

Love in the Age of Google

is love an **abstract noun**
is love a **verb**
is love **actually on Netflix**
is love a **word**

*love is a **temporary madness***
*love is a **hurricane***
*love is a **smoke made with the fume of sighs***
*love is a **losing game***

can love **last forever**
can love break **your heart**
can love2shop **vouchers be used online**
can lovebites **scar**

*love can **build a bridge***
*love can **set you free***
*love can hurt **ed sheeran***
*love cannot **heal me***

does love **cure depression**
does love have **an age**
does lovejoy **marry charlotte**
does love always **fade**

love does not need an explanation
love does not exist
love doesn't need a slogan
love is all there is

Alexa, What is There to Know about Love?

Alexa, what is there to know about love?
What is there to know about love?

A glove is a garment that covers the hand
for protection from the cold or dirt and –

Alexa, how does a human heart work?
How does a human heart work?

Blood is first received in the right atrium via
two veins, the vena cava superior and inferior –

Alexa, where do we go to when we die?
Where do we go to when we die?

Activating Google Maps. Completed activation.
Would you like to start from your current location?

Alexa, what does it mean to be alone?
What does it mean to be alone?

It is the silence left by words unsaid,
the cold expanse of half a bed.

It is the endless stretching of the hours,
the needless tending of plastic flowers.

It is an echo unanswered in a cave,
the fateful ping of the microwave.

It is the fraying of a worn shirt cuff,
and the howl— Alexa, stop! That's enough.

II

Unseen Poem, GCSE English Literature Paper 2

OK. Turn the page. Right, here goes . . .
The first line's straightforward, I suppose.
At least I know what the words all mean.
It has an AA BB rhyming scheme.

What's that French word for when one line
runs into the next? *Jambon*? Never mind.
Susan Jenkins is smiling, I bet she knows.
Oh great! Now the rhymes have disappeared

and the language is getting more caliginous
by the stanza. The voice keeps changing.
At first, it was confident. But now it's ~~confused~~
uncertain (?) and . . . hesitant?

    and as for this bit
        what was the poet even thinking?

    (I can only think
        they must have been drinking)

Susan Jenkins needs more paper.
I hate her. There are ten minutes left.
What's this poem all about anyway?
No idea. I shall just have to guess.

I'll say it's a metaphor for death.

Tsundoku

Tsundoku (noun, Japanese): *the act of acquiring reading materials but letting them pile up in one's home without reading them.*

my bookshelves
used to be tidy
I would dust them
every Friday
and check that
spines aligned
in the sections
I had created
all categories
and genres
carefully curated
and put in order
A-Z by author

Achebe to Zola
went my fiction
and half a shelf
for my diction-
aries and other
reference books
not to mention
the special nook
for first editions
(most of these
in poor condition)
a shelf to gaze
at poems & plays

then rows of lives
dusty histories
of people & places
real-life mysteries
and the section
of learned titles
from economics
to geo-biology
to make me look
quite knowledgy
then comes travel
but it all begins
to unravel

things fall apart
and it breaks
my librarian heart
but it seems
my bookcase
has finally
run out
of space
its dimensions
remain fixed
so books now
just get mixed
I suppose
I could stop
buying books
but I would
much rather
put up with
how it looks

The Reader
Possession
Shame
The Call of the Wild
Chaos: Making a New Science
Disgrace
Decline and Fall
Confessions of a Justified Sinner
Nausea
The Idiot
Les Misérables
Overcoming Obsessive Compulsive Disorder

There's a Supermarket Where Once the Library Stood

There's a supermarket where once the library stood.
I sometimes forget that it's now gone for good.
I asked them last week if they had any Flaubert.
A blank look, then a shrug: 'The cheese counter's there.'

There's a supermarket where once the library had been.
I've been reading the Dahl in 'Indian cuisine'.
No golden tickets, giants, or witches, of course;
just chickpeas and lentils in a creamy spiced sauce.

There's a supermarket where once the library was.
I went in to return an old *Grapes of Wrath*.
'Not a chance,' I was told. It was 'simply too late . . .
they'll be shrivelled and past their best-before date.'

There are supermarkets where once the libraries stood;
they bulldoze their way into new neighbourhoods.
Austerity diets. Towns starved of progress.
Take books off the menu and live well for less.

Ten Rules for Aspiring Poets

1. Poetry does not have to rhyme.
   Well, at least not ~~all the time~~ always.

2. Metaphors can lend a poem power
   (although mixing them isn't good).
   Should they start to fly in all directions,
   nip them in the bud.

3. Focus and concentration
   are important skills to hone.
   Close the door. Turn off the wi-fi.
   Don't get distracted by your ph

4. Avoid clichés like the plague.

5. Don't write stuff that's a bit vague.

6. The use of unnecessarily long words
   may result in reader alienation.
   Curb your sesquipedalianism.
   Obviate all obfuscation.

7. Always proof-read you're work.
   Accuracy can be it's own reward!
   And remember that the penis
   mightier than the sword.

8. Check haiku closely
   for lines which have too few
   or too many syllables.

9. Never ever follow rules.

To Do List

- delay; defer; equivocate
- make some tea; procrastinate
- look at Twitter; stroke the cat
- readjust the thermostat

- dawdle; dither; hem and haw
- fill the kettle; chew my jaw
- write nine words; spin on chair
- play six games of solitaire

- observe the merry, dappled light
  dancing on the page of white
- review my words; paper scrunch
- stroke the cat; break for lunch

- prioritise new tasks to shirk
- ponder changing world of work
- look at Twitter; spin on chair
- make a brew; loiter; stare

- check out latest cricket score
- reorganise the kitchen drawer
- write nine words; cross six out
- stroke the cat; stoke self-doubt

- make tea; stroke cat; cricket; stare
- Twitter; chair-spin; solitaire
- stroke tea; make cat; twicket; wallow
- write To Do list for tomorrow

As Easy as Alpha Bravo Charlie

Aside from all the usual cataclysms,
there is little that fills me with more unease

than the question asked, when on the phone,
'Can you spell that for me, please?'

My knowledge of the NATO phonetic alphabet, you see,
is rather scant and pathetic,

and my attempts to elaborate each letter spelt
unhelpfully unphonetic.

I suppose should take my time. Pause. Think a while.
But no. 'A,' I will blurt out, 'as in . . . *aisle.*'

Or 'That's Bilston with a B,' I sometimes tell them,
'as in the oleo-gum resin, *bdellium.*'

C for *czar*, I might say. Goodness knows why.
I shake my *Djibouti* at D. For E, I say *eye*.

But for F, you would think I could hardly go wrong.
I choose *floccinaucinihilipilification*. Unnecessarily long.

G for *gnashers*. H for *honour*. Neither quite works.
My example for I does nothing but *irk*.

For reasons unclear to me, my J is for *Juan*.
Of all the Ks I could choose, *knee* is the one.

For L, a place-name. But not Lima, oh no.
Llanfairpwllgwyngyllgogerychwyrndrobwllllantysiliogogogoch.

'M,' I will blather, 'as in *mnemonic*.'
People generally *ngwee*, my N is moronic.

O for *Ouija*. No Oscar for me.
My P is *pterodactyl*. For Q, I use *quay*.

Which *right* should they write? My example's a farce.
They must think I'm talking out of my Rs.

'S as in *sea*,' I'll say. Like Canute, I can't hold it back.
My T for *Tchaikovsky*'s a tough nut to crack.

Then there's urn and there's volk; I know they're far-fetchèd.
For W, my choice is utterly *wretched*.

X should be x-ray, but I reference *xylem*;
I wish someone would grant me phonetic asylum.

My Y is for *Yttrium*; my Z, *Zaragoza*.
All useless, unsound. I just shouldn't bother.

Better Never Than Late

It was shortly after I moved into the glasshouse
that I began to throw stones.

Time and tide waited patiently
as I went in search of a badly-fitting cap to wear
and then set off.

Outside, nature was busy admiring a vacuum.
A late-to-rise bird was catching a worm
while overhead, a few of the clouds were lined with silver

and I saw my first swallow of the year.
Summer was here at last.
I could tell that a good day looked in prospect

as an ill wind was blowing. It may have been this
that was responsible for the apples
which had fallen some distance from the tree again.

The bigger they were, the softer they landed.
I imagined the pride they must have felt after they'd fallen.
Before I began to scour for stones,

I checked in on my pre-hatched chickens.
There were five eggs in total. I put them all in my basket;
Granny was coming later and I had promised

to teach her how to suck them. After a brief pause
to smile smugly at my neighbour's yellowing lawn,
I put my second-best foot forward.

Taking the sow's ear silk purse out of my pocket
(all those years I'd spent working as a dentist to gift-horses
had taught me never to come unprepared),

I collected up several large stones,
remembering to roll them down the slope first
to ensure they were completely covered in moss.

I returned home, to where my heart wasn't,
and, being fully consumed by sin, cast the first stone.
It missed by a city mile.

But if a job is worth doing,
it is worth doing to a level of unacceptable mediocrity
and I decided to put off until tomorrow,

what could have been done today.
Wonders ceased and I comforted myself,
not only with the knowledge

that Rome was built in a mere twenty-four hours,
but also with a big slice of cake,
which I both had and ate.

The Bad Salad of William Archibald Spooner

Why do I always watch my birds?
I know that statement sounds absurd
but today I reached an all-lime toe
when I received a blushing crow.

It's wetting gorse – and here's the crunch:
my conversation packs a lunch.
Words stick to my linguistic prying fan.
I think I need a plaster man

to help me when my stouth gets muck.
I could sit, perhaps, and bead a rook,
fight a liar, or flick some powers?
I think I'll go and shake a tower.

Poetic Justice

The poet stood in the dock
looking out upon the court,
as his sentence got metered out.

These things are sent to try us,
he thought.

You have been found guilty
of operating without a valid poetic licence,
declared the judge,
a well-known hard-liner,
scourge of villanelles everywhere.

Words of defiance enjambed
in the poet's throat,
dispossessed of the elegy to fight.
No dramatic monologue
could save him now.

Five cinquains, the judge pronounced
(badly, it must be said),
and the poet's heart sank

although his lawyer reckoned
he could get it reduced
to a couple of quatrains
for good behaviour.

Customers who Bought this Book also Bought

Pikachu Sippy Cup with Straw,
travel mug, 500ml,
made from non-toxic plastic.

Unicorn Healing Meditations,
energetic transmissions and sacred attunements
via Audio CD.

Automatic Bilge Pump,
with 19mm hose barb connection.
Freshwater / saltwater compatible.

Amanda Holden Wall Clock,
pencil drawing print on canvas (large A3),
signed by the artist.

Extendable Selfie Stick,
with wireless remote and tripod stand.
Fluorescent pink.

Hilarious Novelty Christmas Turkey Hat,
made from soft polyester, beige,
63.5 grams, unisex.

V Shape Face Lift Mask & Double Chin Reducer
Collagen gel face with hypoallergenic composition.
Suitable for all chin types.

Inflatable Sumo Costume,
with character style wig.
Battery operated. 100% nylon.

III

Serenity Prayer

Send me a slow news day,
a quiet, subdued day,
in which nothing much happens of note,
just the passing of time,
the consumption of wine,
and a re-run of *Murder, She Wrote*.

Grant me a no news day,
a spare-me-your-views day,
in which nothing much happens at all –
a few hours together,
some regional weather,
a day we can barely recall.

57 Varieties

hard Brexit, soft Brexit, wave-your-arms-aloft Brexit,
quick Brexit, slow Brexit, eat-it-on-the-go Brexit,
smooth Brexit, rough Brexit, creamy-powder-puff Brexit,
best Brexit, worst Brexit, putting-Britain-first Brexit,
fat Brexit, thin Brexit, bear-it-with-a-grin Brexit,
sliced Brexit, ground Brexit, decline-of-the-pound Brexit,
this Brexit, that Brexit, hold-on-to-your-hat Brexit,
black Brexit, white Brexit, Fisher-German-Bight Brexit,
which Brexit, why Brexit, big-bus-with-a-lie Brexit,
rich Brexit, poor Brexit, what-was-life-before Brexit,
wet Brexit, dry Brexit, makes-me-want-to-cry Brexit,
back Brexit, stop Brexit, village-farmhouse-shop Brexit,
brave Brexit, weak Brexit, *Despair*-by-Clinique Brexit,
bruised Brexit, ill Brexit, it's-the-people's-will Brexit,
sharp Brexit, blunt Brexit, Farage-is-a-cunt Brexit,
Tim Brexit, Pam Brexit, pounds-not-kilograms Brexit,
jazz Brexit, soul Brexit, vegan-sausage-roll Brexit,
sheer Brexit, queer Brexit, insert-new-word-here Brexit,
blah Brexit, Brexit Brexit, Brexit-Brexit-Brexit Brexit

Hold my hand and let's jump off this cliff

'Hey! Let's jump off this cliff! It'll be a right laugh!'
urged all the people (well, I mean just over half
of the ones who had bothered to speak up at all).
I peered down at the rocks; it was a long way to fall.

I said, 'But this cliff's more than three hundred feet high
and my doctor tells me if I jump I will die.'
They cried, 'Don't listen to experts. You can trust us.
We read all about it on the side of a bus.'

Unconvinced, I met up with my local MP.
I shared my concerns. He was forced to agree:
'Good heavens! Surely the rocks would smash you to bits!
Why on earth would you go around jumping off cliffs?'

'It was the will of some of the people,' I said
and his expression changed to another instead.
'I think,' he revised, 'you're being melodramatic.
The problem is *you*. You're undemocratic.'

On the clifftop, we waited. In silence we stood.
Then a voice: 'Please remind me why cliff-jumping's good?'
But we just looked down at our shoes, baffled and stumped,
then, out of embarrassment, we held hands

and
jumped.

From the *Encyclopedia of Alternative Facts*

Frankenstein was the *monster*'s name.
There's no such thing as climate change.
A solero is a type of hat.
The planet is not round but flat.

Six is the legal drinking age.
Women get paid an equal wage.
Elvis played keyboards in Take That.
The planet is not round but flat.

Achilles had a dodgy knee.
Terror comes from refugees.
Insomnia affects most cats.
The planet is not round but flat.

Fascism isn't on the rise.
A politician never lies.
It's impossible to change a fact.
The planet is not round but flat.

Penguins

They were sighted off the Dover coast,
drifting in towards the port;
their boat, a snapped-off block of ice,
melting slowly in the warmth.

By the docks, a crowd had formed itself
and congealed into a mob.
Placards were thrust. A chant began.
GO BACK TO WHERE YOU'RE FROM!

'Don't fall for it – they're not displaced,'
declared a spokesman for the right.
'They're only here to take our jobs.
It's as clear as black and white.'

'Tragic,' said the Home Secretary,
as he tried to hide his smirk.
'We'd let them stay but here's the rub –
they lack the paperwork.'

'They'll undermine our way of life,'
said a warning post on Twitter.
'They stink of fish.' 'They'll rape your wife.'
'They got bombs beneath their flippers.'

'BUT WE HAVE NO HOME CLAIMS PENGUIN',
The Sun had printed in disgust.
'And whose fault's THAT – except THEIR OWN?
What's that to do with US?'

The ice had now completely gone.
The penguins battled through the foam,
swimming, swimming, from land to land,
searching for a home.

The White House

He's repainting the White House
in washed-out tones of white:
Pale Shimmer and Frosted Death,
Sour Milk and Clouded Light.

Bleached Lichen in the kitchen;
in the bedrooms, Faded Tan;
Pure White in the Oval Office:
the new range from the Du Lux Klan.

Bird Watching

I spot him near the precinct,
plumage distinct

by its raggedness,
a grey-coated shabbiness

worn through all weathers,
feet time-withered

in their splay-toed shuffle.
He grubs on, unruffled

by retail footfall,
past the market stalls,

lucky-dipping in litter bins
for gold and glittered things,

and some lunch,
a grease-smeared treasure hunt

among burger wrappers and coffee cups.
Meanwhile those higher up

in the order of pecking,
stick their necks in,

keep their beaks out,
find a less shamefaced route.

I take flight, too. A sudden lurch,
a few flaps, and I'm perched

on a gargoyle, west side of St Hugh's:
throne of sky, a bird's eye view.

Up here, I'm lord of everything.
I polish my feathers, clean my wings.

Below, I see him outside M&S,
his sleeping bag, a quilted nest.

Metrics

Totally SMASHED it. A new PB:
10K run in **46.13**.
This time, I chose to go a different route
to avoid the homeless outside Boots:
the Slalom of the Sleeping Bags, I reckon,
costs me several precious seconds.

Last night I had **8.5 hours** of sleep
(down **30 mins** on my stats last week).
I'd have slept longer – maybe two hours more –
if not for the sobbing from next door.
Oh, the broken nights I have known.
She often screams when her husband's home.

Social media helps me unwind.
A quick check-in to my stats online:
46 new Instagram fans;
85 likes for my fitness plan;
selfie retweets, a meagre **15**
(a **2.6 drop** in my self-esteem).

Life's to be measured. Metrics help me
to be the best I can possibly be.
That's **12,000 steps** I've taken today
(and **600 calories** blasted away!):
impressive stats that deserve to be shared,
to walk so far and not go anywhere.

An Update to My Privacy Policy

I have updated my Privacy Policy
as part of my ongoing commitment
to not being found,

using simple-to-understand language,
such as *'please go away'*
and *'just leave me alone'*.

I will not share myself with third parties,
dinner parties or fancy dress parties.
For offers of free biscuits,

please consult my Cookie Policy.
My privacy is important to me
as is this duvet.

You are receiving this poem
because you have expressed an interest
in receiving this poem.

Please know that you can unsubscribe
from this poem at any time,
by clicking here.

Mrs Fatima Sabah Abdallah

I

Dear Mrs Fatima Sabah Abdallah,

Thank you very much for your massage,
which, as you so correctly predicted,
has come as a surprise to me.

I was sorry to learn of the death of your husband,
following his long and illustrious career
as an international oil merchant.

I, too, pray for a day when there will be
more stringent health and safety regulations
in the jet ski and leisure watercraft industry.

For you to receive such a diagnosis,
so shortly after your late husband's accident,
leaves me little wonder that you should write to me
with heavy sorrow in your heart:
three weeks is not a long time.

It is to your great credit
you can yet find it within yourself
to praise GOD ALMIGHTY with such abundance
(I counted six times),

and more noble still,
your decision to devote your family savings –
the quite Magnificent Sum, as you say,
of Four Million, Seven Hundred Thousand Pounds Only,
earned through the Hard, Honest Sweat
of your late husband's labours –
to the pursuit of Charitable Works.

Your BUSINESS PROPOSITION of 40 percent of the total monies
for my own personal use
to help you bring your project to fruition
is indeed a Kind and Generous one.

But I am afraid I must decline,
not wishing to divert funds away
from the establishment of your new Orphanage
which, as you rightly say, would be
a Most Humble and Worthy Memorial
to the late Mr Abdallah.

II

Dear Mrs Abdallah,

Thank you for your latest massage.
While a Thousand Flowers have yet to Bloom in my Garden,
there are signs here that Spring is on its way:
there is celandine in the hedgerows,
the skylark is in good voice.

How sorry I am to learn
of the Deterioration in your Health Condition.
I see you continue to draw strength
from GOD ALMIGHTY (seven times, in fact)
and I do hope the dramatic recovery
of your late husband's jet ski
provides some comfort in your final days.

Thank you also for the photographs
of orphaned children
and the blueprint of the architect's plans.

The Revised Terms of your Business Proposition are tempting
but I am afraid I cannot supply you
with my bank details at this time.

III

Dear Fatima (if I may),

Thank you again for your recent kind words.
Although my Sweet and Blessed Footsteps
are not currently Strewn with Rose Petals as you had hoped,
the bumblebees buzz purposefully,
and the cherry blossom bursts forth.

Following the latest news of your Health Condition,
I said a prayer for you to GOD ALMIGHTY.
I agree it now seems unlikely
that we might meet before your Departure
from this Glorious Mother Earth.

But how happy you looked
in the photograph attached to your last massage,
with your hair blowing in the wind,
as you roared into harbour,
like Aphrodite riding in upon the sea foam.

And that's splendid news about the orphanage.
My bank details are enclosed.

IV

My dearest Fatima,

I write to you with no expectation of reply.
Here, Summer has breathed its last
and the October winds have begun to weave
golden carpets upon the ground.

I wanted you to know
that I have invested my half of the funds
from your Fair and Honest Business Proposition
to continue the Most Excellent Charitable Works
that you have begun.

A photograph is attached.
From it, you will see building work is finished
and the first children have begun to arrive.
They come with nothing in their rucksacks
but rocks and hope.
Mr Abdallah would be proud of all you have achieved.

I hope this massage finds the two of you united once again,
and each Sweet and Blessed footstep
you take together
to be Strewn with Rose Petals,

while you make your way through the garden
of your one and only GOD ALMIGHTY,
in which, I like to imagine,
a Thousand Flowers have Bloomed.

Please Read These Instructions Carefully

The operation is much easier to complete
when performed by two people.
Check for compatibility before commencement.

Do not attempt when under the influence of alcohol.
All components must be well lubricated (see enclosed booklet).
Batteries are not included.

Ensure measures are in place to minimise
the risk of accident. It is recommended
to always use the protective gear provided.

Insert Screw Rod into opening (A)
until flush with the body, as indicated in diagram C.
Note: exterior may differ depending on the model.

Lower your hips back to the starting position
and repeat for the desired number of repetitions.
Prioritise a straight line from your knees.

For other permutations,
including adjustment to a fully extendable position,
please see pages 12–16.

If you feel symptoms such as tingling,
numbness, burning or stiffness, stop and rest
for several hours before resuming.

Remember to take a 10 to 15 minute break every hour,
even if you don't think you need it.
Your driving reaction time may be affected.

Upon completion, wipe away any liquids
which may have appeared with a soft, damp cloth.
DO NOT use an abrasive cleaner.

You should repeat as necessary
until symptoms subside
or your doctor instructs you otherwise.

Please store these instructions in a safe place.
You may need them for future reference.

ee cummings attempts online banking

Now enter a password.
i carry your heart with me

Spaces are not allowed. Please try again.
icarryyourheartwithme

Passwords must contain at least one special character.
Please try again.
icarryyourheartwithme(icarryitinmyheart)

Password must not contain more than 21 characters.
Please try again.
icarryyourear(withme)

Passwords must contain a mix of alpha-numeric characters.
Please try again.
1carryy0urear(w1thme)

Passwords need to contain at least one uppercase letter.
Please try again.

Passwords need to contain at least one uppercase letter.
Please try again.

This page is about to expire.
Please enter your new password.

Password(123)

Composition

The human body
is sixty per cent water,
he read

and he sat there,
silent, frowning,

wondering
whether that was why
he always felt

as if he was
slowly drowning.

IV

Lonely Hearts

I
Woman, thrice widowed,
seeks man for love, sex, marriage,
and possibly more.

II
Thrifty M, 40,
ISO LTR with
W, 40.

III
Chickpea fanatic
seeks similar. Requirements:
good sense of humous.

IV
Herb-loving woman
looking to find her Basil.
No thyme-wasters, please.

V
Doll needs puppeteer
for a night of jiggling
with no strings attached.

VI
Haiku debutante,
with a fondness for rambling,
would like to meet a

VII
Ex-librarian,
available for lending.
Take me off the shelf.

VIII
Hieroglyphist seeks
illegible bachelor
for late-night doodles.

IX
Sarcy pessimist
seeks man to brighten the days.
Yeah, like he exists.

First Date

We'd so much in common, that was clear from the start:
a marriage of souls, like de Beauvoir and Sartre.
The connection was instant, almost irrational:
simply simpatico, fully compatible.

You confessed you loved winter, North Yorkshire, and cats.
'Me, too!' I responded. 'How amazing is that?'
You were wild about Wharton: you loved *Ethan Frome*.
'His best,' I said, thinking I'd read him when home.

You praised a revival of Pinter's *Dumb Waiter*.
I nodded along. I should google that later.
The discussion then turned to things that you hated:
Tarantino, you thought, was quite over-rated.

'You make some good points,' I eventually said.
I could always hide that box set under my bed.
You spoke of a loathing of poetry that rhymed
and I said yes,
that stuff's awful.

Meet Cute

was a term I encountered by chance,
when skimming channels one night,
and bumping into it

in a documentary about romcoms.
It was a staple scene of the genre, I learnt;
quite possibly the key scene –

the one where boy meets girl
for the very first time,
or boy meets boy, or girl meets girl

(other permutations are available),
amidst some hilarious misunderstanding
or imbroglio,

neither suspecting that this was the Big One,
the Knockout, the Life-changer.
Think of that ill-advised road trip

of Harry and Sally's; or Julia Roberts,
wearing shades and a beret,
and half of Hugh Grant's orange juice.

And now, having a name for it,
it makes me wonder
whether all those awkward brushes

and misunderstandings in my own life
were simply meet cutes
that I'd failed to recognise:

all those upturned coffee cups
and unhurdled bags,
the fingertips which met while groping

for the corner shop's last loaf.
Not to mention, one hundred other close encounters
of the romcom kind,

featuring a whole cast of leading ladies,
who, disappointed with the lack of chemistry,
would tear up the scripts

as soon as the scene was finished,
and head off in search
of more compelling co-stars

with whom to film their biopics.
And then I think of how we met
and I'm reassured

that real life is not a Hollywood movie,
that romance need not begin
with a set-to or a spillage

but a simple hello
and a look between two people,
and which may be a collision, nonetheless.

An Exchange of Similes

Your beauty, I said,
is like the existence of climate change:
undeniable.

My presence, you said,
is like the 8.14 to London Paddington:
unreliable.

Your eyes, I said,
are like Birmingham's Municipal Baths:
made to swim in.

My waist, you said,
is like a garden hedge that impedes pedestrians when they walk
    past:
in need of trimming.

Your lips, I said,
are like an obstructive snooker ball:
asking to be kissed.

My words, you said,
are like an out-of-form batsman:
easily dismissed.

Your hair, I said,
is like a new series of keep-fit books:
shiny, healthy and volumized.

My dress sense, you said,
is like agriculture in nineteenth-century Tsarist Russia:
primitive and unmodernised.

Your skin, I said,
is like Gary Lineker's disciplinary record:
without blemish.

My voice, you said,
is like a painting by Peter Paul Rubens:
oily and phlegmish.

Your legs, I said,
are like this line of my poem when you compare it to all the other
    lines in my poem:
long.

My taste in music, you said,
is like the inclusion of this semi-colon;
wrong.

Your body, I said,
is like the mysterious ocean deep:
worth exploring.

My conversation, you said,
is like a pneumatic drill:
boring.

Your chest, I said,
is like a luxury penthouse suite:
palatial and roomy.

I, you said,
am like a large plate glass window:
you see right me through me.

A coming together such as ours, I said,
is a rare celestial event,
like a supernova.

Forget it, you said,
our relationship is like this poem:
over.

Remembrance of Things Pasta

She blew her fusilli,
my pretty penne,
when she found me watching
daytime tagliatelle.

Je ne spaghetti rien,
I responded in song,
but she did not linguini
for long,

just walked out
without further retort:
a hard lesson to be tortellini,
orzo I thought.

And so here I am,
all on my macaroni,
and now my days
feel cannelloni.

On Finding Myself within the Pages of
a Mills & Boon Novel

Even the beautiful but feisty Ellie Forbes
could not help but feel a little overawed

at the sight of his famous satinwood writing desk.
Ruggedly, he swivelled round, feeling her breath

on his broad, manly shoulder. Ellie kept her head.
'So this is where the magic happens,' she said

attractively, as her vibrant, auburn hair, still damp
from her swim, shone in the glow of his reading lamp.

The poet laureate raised an eyebrow ruggedly
and Ellie wondered if she'd overstepped the mark. Suddenly,

he smiled and the dark and brooding features
of his face relented to something sunnier. He was a genius,

they said. But could she ever love a poet again?
She remembered Gerald and his awful cinquains.

No, she mustn't, she told herself and made to leave.
'Don't go. Stay for a while,' he said sternly. 'Please,'

he added, his rugged face softening once more.
'It's this poem.' He opened his felt-lined desk drawer

and handed it to her, and again his brow furrowed.
'It's for the royal wedding tomorrow.

I need a rhyme for orange but I'm stuck.'
'Well, Mr Poet Laureate, it seems you're in luck,'

she teased, reaching over him with a coquettish wink,
dipping his nib into the thick, black ink.

The Unrequited Love of an Olympic Pole Vaulter

I guess
it wasn't
meant
to be

your bar
was set
too high
for me

it's been
four years
since we
last met

and I
haven't
got over
you yet

My Heart is a Lump of Rock

Rewrite the textbooks if you please,
the scientists are on their knees.
Doctors, I'm told, are still in shock:
my heart is just a lump of rock.

It used to function rather well,
(at least as far as I could tell),
It did its job of pumping blood
and other things a good heart should.

It sometimes raced or skipped a beat
(whenever you and I would meet)
but since the day that you took off,
my heart has been a lump of rock.

Geologists are at my door
to see if they can find out more.
It's igneous, they think, in part,
this love-cooled rock that's called my heart.

Eye Chart for the Optically Deluded

O

U R

L O V E

IS NOT BLIND

JUST A LITTLE

SHORT SIGHTED

MY FEELINGS FOR YOU

ARE STILL UNREQUITED

HOW I WISH YOU COULD SEE

CAN YOU NOT TAKE A HINT

YOU HAVE OPENED MY EYES

NOW PLEASE READ THE SMALL PRINT

Might Have, Might Not Have

I might have taken an earlier train.
You might not have had reason to catch it.
Your boss might have chosen somebody else.
You might not have selected that carriage.

I might have decided to travel by bus.
You might not have answered his call.
The snow which fell might have been the wrong kind.
The train might not have pulled up at all.

The Beeching Report might have closed this line.
The Steam Age might not have occurred.
George Stephenson's Rocket might have misfired.
I might not have found the right words.

I might have just stood in the vestibule.
That man might not have moved his briefcase.
You might have slept, not flashed me a smile.
Worlds might not have collided in space.

The way things happen.
And the way things don't.
The way things fall into place.

The News Where I Am

Today, my travelcard expired.
Got soaked through twice. Oh, and got fired.
A dog bit me. I lost my phone
   but
      you'll be there when I get home.

A pigeon crapped upon my head.
I ate a slice of mouldy bread.
I lost a tooth. I broke three bones.
   Who cares?
      You'll be there when I get home.

My lottery numbers came up today
(a shame that I forgot to play).
I think I've got a kidney stone.
   Like, whatever.
      You'll be there when I get home.

The icecaps melt some more each year.
A new world war will soon be here.
The most perfect day that I've known!
   Because
      – did I mention this? –
         you'll be there when I get home.

Early Morning Symphony

Those blasted birds are at it again,
singing about you at 6 a.m.,

forcing me up to make the tea,
down the staircase that creaks

your name to the kitchen.
There's music there, too. I listen

to the gushing of the taps
and, after the lighting of the gas,

the kettle begins to croon
its familiar, ancient tune,

as old as love itself, this song.
You, snoring. Me, whistling along,

what a symphony this is!
And listen . . . there's the fridge

joining in, humming gently,
not yet even half-empty.

Wedding Anniversary

I forgot, I said,
but since when was our love built
on anything so ordinary
as a date?

Let other couples mark time.
I am too caught up
with the here and the now of you
to waste these hours

in commemoration of the past.
Because our love is vast,
like an ocean,
with depths far beyond

others' comprehension.
Why spend our lives swimming circles
in the muddy puddle
of convention?

Flowers fade.
Chocolates get eaten.
By such ephemera,
we should judge our love not.

And you said,
what do you mean,
you *forgot*?

How to Tell the Difference between Larkspur and Delphiniums

There are times when I wish I could be
one of those of proper poets,
of the kind who have the language of nature
at their green and bucolic fingertips.

You know the sort of thing they write:
some suitably verdant words
about the eroticism of moss;
or how beauty is as frail

as a robin's speckled egg;
or some metaphor, quickly tossed off,
about the fecundity
of hollyhocks.

But I never learnt that language;
the words never quite stuck
to the pictures somehow
and the oaks

and the elms and beeches,
all look the same to me.
Brown trunks, green leaves.
Quite tall, as a rule.

And should I describe you in other terms:
as a sublime cover drive,
as a perfect middle eight,
or an expertly pulled pint of Guinness

from the pub on the way back home,
that's because these are things
I press between the pages
of my own Arcadian nature-book,

things that fill me with joy,
and that I'm probably thinking about
when you tell me –
for what must be the hundredth time –

how to tell the difference
between larkspur and delphiniums.

In Absentia

Since you left, the house has fallen
into chronic disrepair.

The sink is piled with pots and pans.
Bugs are eating the armchair

in which I sit and watch the paint
as it peels itself from the wall.

There's a damp patch on the ceiling.
Dry rot creeps up through the floor

and an emptiness spreads itself
across the room, our house, my life,

like margarine on mouldy bread
smeared from an unclean knife.

I need to find the strength to rise
and to put the kettle on,

wash up and get the table laid;
I hope the queue is not too long.

It's six minutes now since you left
for milk, a loaf, and free-range eggs.

She'd Dance

She'd dance like no one was watching
although she liked to think he was.
The kitchen was her grand ballroom;
her partner was a mop.

She'd foxtrot among the pots and pans,
she'd paso doble to the sink,
and as she swept across the floor,
her mind danced, too. She'd think

of how he'd held her in his arms
at the Locarno and the Ritz –
whirling, waltzing, a world apart –
in the years before the kids,

and longer still before the shadow
the doctor spotted on his lungs.
How dazzlingly they had danced!
How dizzyingly she had spun!

Her neighbours saw her sometimes,
shuffling bent-backed to the shops.
But at home, she'd dance like no one was watching
although she liked to think he was.

Gun Fight in the Last Chance Saloon

Now we are old but not quite dead,
not knowing if today might be our last,
We could devote ourselves to jigsaws
and to *Remembrance of Things Past*.

Yes, that would be a blast.

I couldn't think of anything worse.
Why act as if we're already in the hearse
when we've still got time to run amok,
to cause a stir, to shake and shock

our po-faced neighbours
when they find our photo in the papers,
caught by the cops with our knickers down
in a disused warehouse
on the wrong side of town,

having first taken out a gang of thugs
in a brawl over a consignment
of non-recreational drugs.
We would have gotten away with it, too,
if it wasn't for my back and your arthritis.

Or, then again . . .

we could get out of bed at half-past ten,
and have breakfast on the patio
if the weather's good. I could mow the lawn,
and you could prune the roses then –
hang on, stop . . .

please, excuse me while I yawn.

It's a sort of life but only just
and it won't be long until we're dust
so let's think big, go large, be bold,
we're not dead yet, we're only old

and there's time left still
for us to lead the revolution.
We can become saboteurs with secateurs,
and cut off the supply lines
of tyrants and dictators.

We can spray slug repellent
in the faces of racists and fascists,
and plunder our allotment
to pelt perpetrators of prejudice
with mouldy spuds and cabbages.

Or, I suppose . . .

we could live out our last days in repose,
filling in crosswords and the hours.
Let the quiz shows exert their daily pull.
We'd drift in and out on time's tide:
how peaceful that all sounds

and how dull.

That's not my idea of fun.
But a life of crime spent on the run:
now, there's a life I could abide.
We could be a doddery Bonnie and Clyde

and hold up banks
by depositing a lifetime's worth of coppers
from our penny jars.
We'd use our mobility scooters
as getaway cars

and spread panic on the pavements
with our drive-by tootings.
We'd find a hideout to store our loot in,
one with a stairlift preferably,
what with my hip and your dodgy knee.

But hang on . . .

there, in the hedge, there's something moving.
Behind the old pear tree, a sudden glint.
A bush that wasn't there yesterday.
We're surrounded. It must be time, I think.

You grab that walking-stick.
I'll take my chances with the brolly.
On the count of three, let's burst out the door
and give them all we've got.

You and me, kid,

One –

against the world,

Two –

just like it always was.

Three –